STEAM

Module for Teachers

STEAM

Module for Teachers

UNBOUND SCRIPT

STEAM MODULE FOR TEACHERS

ISBN : 978-81-19745-50-0

Publisher
Unbound Script
B-10, Seven Wonder Business Center
Plot No. G-20, Basement, Preet Vihar
New Delhi-110092
Website : www.unboundscript.com
Email : books@unboundscript.com

Compilation & Illustration - Unbound Script

Price: ₹ 450/-

Printed in India

PREFACE

Welcome to the journey of **STEAM** education—a dynamic approach to teaching and learning that integrates **Science, Technology, Engineering, Arts,** and **Mathematics** to inspire creativity, innovation, and problem-solving in the classroom. As educators, you play a pivotal role in shaping the minds and futures of the next generation. With this handbook, we aim to provide you with valuable insights, resources, and strategies to effectively implement **STEAM** practices in your teaching practice. **STEAM** education transcends traditional boundaries, fostering interdisciplinary connections and empowering students to explore the world through a lens of curiosity and inquiry. In this handbook, you will find practical tips for designing **STEAM** lessons, integrating technology into the curriculum, and facilitating hands-on, experiential learning experiences.

Through the pages of this handbook, we invite you to embark on a journey of exploration, discovery, and transformation. Together, let us inspire the next generation of innovators, problem-solvers, and lifelong learners through the power of **STEAM** education.

Contents

UNDERSTAND STEAM

What is STEAM?

In recent years, education has witnessed a transformative approach known as STEAM - an acronym for Science, Technology, Engineering, Arts, and Mathematics. STEAM represents a holistic educational philosophy that integrates these traditionally separate disciplines into a cohesive framework. It's more than just an amalgamation of subjects; it's a catalyst for creativity, innovation, and problem-solving in the modern world.

At its core, STEAM recognizes the interconnectedness of these disciplines and emphasizes their application in real-world contexts. By incorporating arts into the traditional STEM subjects (Science, Technology, Engineering, and Mathematics), STEAM education transcends the boundaries of conventional learning, fostering a dynamic environment where students can explore, experiment, and create.

Science provides the foundation for inquiry and discovery, encouraging students to ask questions, conduct experiments, and make observations about the natural world. Technology empowers students to leverage tools and resources to solve problems, develop digital literacy skills, and explore emerging fields such as coding and robotics.

Engineering embodies the spirit of innovation and design thinking, challenging students to tackle complex problems, prototype solutions, and engage in hands-on projects that simulate real-world engineering challenges. Arts, often regarded as the soul of STEAM, inspire creativity, expression, and interdisciplinary connections. Through visual arts, music, theater, and more, students can unleash their imagination, cultivate empathy, and communicate ideas in innovative ways.

Mathematics serves as the universal language of STEAM, providing the framework for logical reasoning, pattern recognition, and quantitative analysis. From geometry to calculus, mathematical concepts permeate every aspect of STEAM education, reinforcing critical thinking skills and problem-solving strategies.

Together, these disciplines form the foundation of STEAM education, empowering students to become lifelong learners, innovative thinkers, and global citizens. By embracing the STEAM approach, educators can nurture a generation of individuals equipped with the skills, knowledge, and creativity to thrive in an ever-evolving world.

In this chapter, we'll explore the principles, practices, and benefits of STEAM education, highlighting its transformative impact on teaching and learning. From inspiring classroom anecdotes to cutting-edge research, we'll uncover the power of STEAM to ignite curiosity, unlock potential, and shape the future of education.

THE BENEFITS OF A STEAM APPROACH

There are as many benefits to STEAM approaches, as there are approaches to STEAM around the world!

STEAM Approaches aim to be:

- Creative
- Interdisciplinary / Transdisciplinary
- Flexible
- Relevant to the Learners
- Inclusive
- Hands-on
- Participatory
- Fun!

The overall aspiration is to facilitate better understanding in, and empowerment of, the learner. But the specific purpose of STEAM approaches is very much dependent on the context. As such every organisation, educator and learner will apply the approach and experience the benefits in different ways.

STEAM Approaches aim to engage:

- Creativity
- Critical Thinking Skills
- Curiosity
- Change of Attitude to Learning
- Collaboration Skills
- Confidence
- Communication

5 PILLARS of STEAM:

- Steam orchestrated by a teacher
- Balancing skills and knowledge
- Modern methodologies and their relation with STEAM?
- Problems to be solved are situated within realistic contexts
- Assessment

STEAM: Orchestrated by a Teacher

STEAM, an acronym standing for Science, Technology, Engineering, Arts, and Mathematics, represents an interdisciplinary approach to education that integrates these subjects into a cohesive learning paradigm. While STEAM initiatives are often associated with schools, they can be orchestrated by teachers, administrators, or educational institutions seeking to foster innovation, creativity, and critical thinking among students.

1. **Curriculum Integration:** Teachers can integrate STEAM concepts into their existing lesson plans across various subjects. For example, a science teacher might incorporate art projects into biology lessons, encouraging students to create models of cells or ecosystems. Similarly, a math teacher might explore geometric principles through engineering design projects.
2. **Cross-Disciplinary Projects:** Teachers can design collaborative projects that require students to draw upon knowledge from multiple disciplines. For instance, a project to design and build a solar-powered vehicle would involve

elements of science (understanding solar energy), technology (building the vehicle), engineering (designing the structure), arts (aesthetics and design), and mathematics (calculating energy efficiency and dimensions).

3. **Hands-On Activities:** Implementing hands-on activities and experiments is crucial in STEAM education. Teachers can organize lab sessions, maker space activities, or coding workshops to provide students with practical experiences that reinforce theoretical concepts.

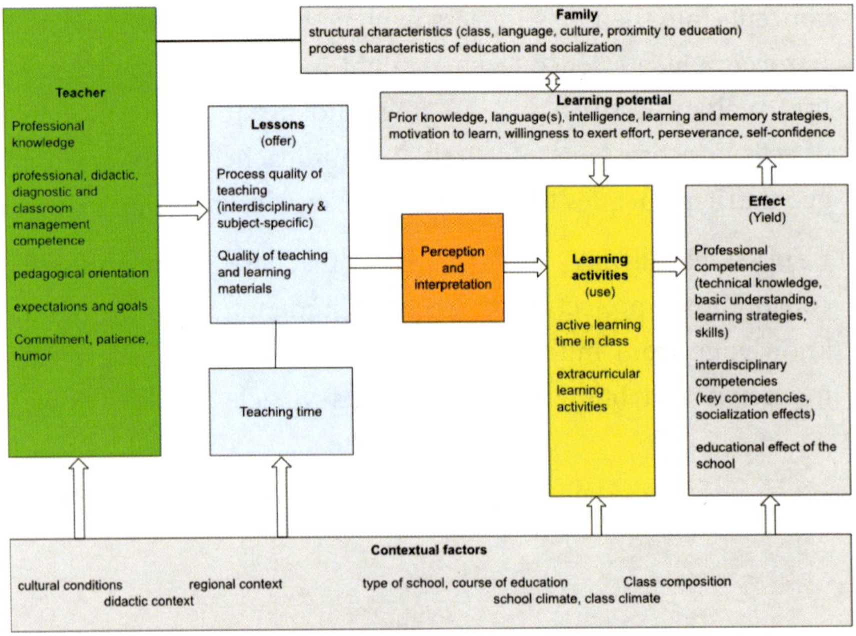

4. **Problem-Based Learning:** Teachers can present students with real-world problems or challenges that require STEAM skills to solve. This approach encourages critical thinking, problem-solving, and collaboration. For example, students might be tasked with designing a sustainable urban environment or creating an interactive art installation using technology.
5. **Guest Speakers and Field Trips:** Inviting professionals from STEM or arts fields to speak to students can provide valuable insights into real-world applications of STEAM concepts. Additionally, organizing field trips to museums, science centers, or tech companies can expose students to STEAM-related careers and industries.
6. **Technology Integration:** Leveraging technology such as 3D printers, robotics kits, or computer software can enhance STEAM learning experiences. Teachers can incorporate tools like CAD software for engineering design projects or programming languages for coding activities.
7. **Assessment and Reflection:** Teachers can assess student learning through a variety of methods, including project presentations, portfolio reviews, or written reflections. Encouraging students to reflect on their learning process fosters metacognition and helps them recognize the connections between different disciplines.

8. **Community Engagement:** Engaging parents, local businesses, and community organizations can enrich STEAM education initiatives. Teachers can collaborate with these stakeholders to provide mentorship opportunities, secure resources, or organize community events showcasing student projects.

By orchestrating STEAM education in these ways, teachers play a vital role in preparing students for the challenges and opportunities of the 21st century, equipping them with the skills and mindset necessary for success in an increasingly complex and interconnected world.

Balancing skills & knowledge (brains on, hands on)

STEAM education emphasizes a balanced approach between theoretical knowledge (often referred to as "brains on") and practical, hands-on application of that knowledge. This holistic approach ensures that students not only understand concepts intellectually but also develop the skills needed to apply them in real-world contexts. Here's how STEAM achieves this balance:

1. **Theoretical Understanding (Brains On):**
    - STEAM education begins with a solid foundation in core concepts across science, technology, engineering, arts, and mathematics. Teachers facilitate learning through lectures, discussions, readings, and multimedia resources to ensure students grasp theoretical knowledge.

- Students engage in critical thinking, problem-solving, and analytical reasoning to understand the underlying principles behind various phenomena and concepts.

2. Practical Application (Hands On):

- Hands-on activities, experiments, and projects are integral components of STEAM education. These activities provide students with opportunities to apply theoretical knowledge in practical settings.
- By engaging in hands-on projects, students develop essential skills such as creativity, collaboration, communication, and resilience. They learn to work through challenges, troubleshoot problems, and iterate on their designs or solutions.

3. Project-Based Learning:

- STEAM education often employs project-based learning (PBL) methodologies, where students work on extended, interdisciplinary projects that require them to integrate knowledge and skills from multiple disciplines.
- Through PBL, students tackle authentic, real-world problems or challenges, which not only deepen their understanding of concepts but also foster a sense of ownership and relevance in their learning.

4. Experiential Learning:

- Experiential learning is central to the hands-on component of STEAM education. This approach emphasizes learning by doing, where students actively engage with materials, tools, and technologies to explore concepts and phenomena.

- Whether conducting experiments in a science lab, programming robots, designing prototypes, or creating works of art, students gain valuable experiential learning experiences that reinforce theoretical concepts.

5. **Reflection and Iteration:**
   - In STEAM education, reflection is an essential component of the learning process. Students reflect on their hands-on experiences, analyze outcomes, and identify areas for improvement.
   - Through reflection, students develop metacognitive skills, gaining insights into their learning process and understanding how to refine their approaches for future projects or challenges.

By balancing theoretical knowledge with hands-on application, STEAM education cultivates well-rounded learners who not only possess a deep understanding of academic concepts but also have the practical skills and abilities needed to succeed in a rapidly evolving world.

Modern methodologies and their relation with STEAM?

Modern methodologies in education often align closely with the principles of STEAM (Science, Technology, Engineering, Arts, and Mathematics) education, as they emphasize active learning, interdisciplinary approaches, and the development of critical thinking and problem-solving skills. Here are several modern methodologies and their relationship with STEAM:

1. **Project-Based Learning (PBL):**

- PBL is a student-centered approach where students learn by engaging in real-world projects that require them to investigate and solve complex problems.
- Relation with STEAM: PBL is inherently interdisciplinary, making it well-suited for STEAM education. Students collaborate across disciplines to tackle authentic problems, integrating knowledge and skills from science, technology, engineering, arts, and mathematics.

2. **Inquiry-Based Learning:**

- Inquiry-based learning encourages students to ask questions, explore topics, and construct their understanding through hands-on investigation and experimentation.
- Relation with STEAM: Inquiry-based learning fosters curiosity and critical thinking, essential skills in STEAM fields. Students engage in scientific inquiry, technological exploration, and creative experimentation, aligning with the interdisciplinary nature of STEAM education.

3. **Design Thinking:**

- Design thinking is a problem-solving methodology that emphasizes empathy, ideation, prototyping, and testing to address complex challenges.
- Relation with STEAM: Design thinking aligns closely with the engineering and creative aspects of STEAM education. Students apply design thinking principles to develop innovative solutions, integrating scientific knowledge with artistic expression and technological innovation.

4. **Flipped Classroom:**

- In a flipped classroom, students learn foundational content outside of class through videos or readings, allowing class time to be used for active learning activities and discussions.

- Relation with STEAM: Flipped classrooms provide opportunities for hands-on, collaborative learning experiences in STEAM subjects. Class time can be devoted to project work, experimentation, and application of concepts, fostering deeper engagement and understanding.

5. **Collaborative Learning:**

- Collaborative learning emphasizes group work and peer interaction, where students learn from one another through discussion, cooperation, and shared problem-solving.
- Relation with STEAM: Collaboration is essential in STEAM education, where students often work in teams to tackle interdisciplinary challenges. Collaborative learning environments encourage knowledge sharing, diverse perspectives, and the development of communication and teamwork skills.

6. **Maker Education:**

- Maker education emphasizes hands-on, experiential learning through making, tinkering, and creating using tools, materials, and technologies.
- Relation with STEAM: Maker education is closely aligned with the hands-on aspect of STEAM education. Students engage in design, prototyping, and fabrication activities, integrating concepts from science, technology, engineering, arts, and mathematics while fostering creativity and innovation.

Overall, modern methodologies in education promote active learning, interdisciplinary approaches, and the development of 21st-century skills, making them highly compatible with the principles of STEAM education. These methodologies provide students with opportunities to explore, create, and innovate, preparing them for success in an increasingly complex and interconnected world.

Element	Description	Ask Yourself
Topic	Project-based learning planning is similar to planning a unit of study. You'll need to choose a topic that students can explore and ask questions about.	What topics are the students in my class interested in?
Content	The main reason to use PBL is to teach standard-driven content. Before you can plan a PBL, you must know which standards you want students to apply to their project.	Which standards fit well with the topic I've chosen?
Driving Question	The "driving question" is the overall question students will explore in the project. They will gain and apply knowledge to answer this question. The skills used to complete the project are driven by the standards.	What end result do I want to see from my students?
In-Depth Inquiry & choice	Students will use resources (including ones you provide and ones they seek out) to ask and answer questions. Project-based learning should allow for students to make choices that will create a different outcome for each student.	What process do I want students to complete in order to answer the driving question? What resources do I need to provide and what resources will they seek out on their own? What choices will my students make?
Critique and Revision	Students will need to give and receive feedback throughout the PBL. They will make several revisions and do further research to improve their projects.	During which parts of the project will I have students share their work? How will they share their work? How will I explicitly teach revision of their work?
Public Audience/ Final product	Students will present their project to an audience other than the teacher and classmates. This can include other grade levels, community members, and/or family members.	Who would benefit from learning about my students' work?
21st century competencies	Within the project, students will work on skills related to real life. These skills include collaboration, problem solving, communication, innovation, and technology use.	How can I explicitly teach 21st century competencies? How will students then apply these competencies?

Problems to be solved are situated within realistic contexts

In STEAM education, problems are often situated within realistic or authentic contexts to enhance student engagement, relevance, and application of learning. By presenting challenges that mirror real-world scenarios, students are encouraged to apply their knowledge and skills in meaningful ways. Here are several examples of problems situated within realistic/authentic contexts in STEAM education:

1. **Designing Sustainable Solutions:**
   - Problem: Students are tasked with designing sustainable solutions to address environmental challenges, such as reducing plastic waste or improving energy efficiency.
   - Context: The problem is situated within the context of environmental conservation and sustainable development, reflecting real-world concerns about climate change and resource depletion.
2. **Creating Assistive Technologies:**
   - Problem: Students are challenged to design and prototype assistive technologies to improve the quality of life for individuals with disabilities.
   - Context: The problem is situated within the context of healthcare and accessibility, addressing real-world needs for innovative solutions to support people with disabilities in their daily lives.

3. **Urban Planning and Design:**
    - Problem: Students are tasked with designing and planning a sustainable urban community that promotes livability, equity, and environmental stewardship.
    - Context: The problem is situated within the context of urban development and city planning, addressing real-world challenges related to population growth, infrastructure, and urbanization.
4. **Innovating for Social Change:**
    - Problem: Students are challenged to develop innovative solutions to address social issues such as poverty, inequality, or access to education.
    - Context: The problem is situated within the context of social entrepreneurship and civic engagement, empowering students to make a positive impact in their communities.
5. **Exploring Space Exploration Challenges:**
    - Problem: Students are tasked with designing and building a prototype for a spacecraft or rover to explore a specific celestial body, such as Mars or the Moon.
    - Context: The problem is situated within the context of space exploration and technology, reflecting real-world endeavors by space agencies and private companies to explore and colonize other planets.
6. **Addressing Global Health Challenges:**
    - Problem: Students are challenged to develop strategies to address global health challenges, such as disease prevention, access to healthcare, or vaccine distribution.

- Context: The problem is situated within the context of public health and global development, highlighting real-world issues that impact communities worldwide.

By situating problems within realistic or authentic contexts, STEAM education fosters relevance, engagement, and application of learning. Students are encouraged to think critically, collaborate with peers, and apply their knowledge and skills to solve complex problems that have tangible implications in the real world.

Assessment

Assessment in STEAM education aims to evaluate students' understanding of interdisciplinary concepts, their ability to apply knowledge and skills across multiple disciplines, and their proficiency in problem-solving, critical thinking, and creativity. Here are several approaches to assessment commonly used in STEAM education:

1. Project-Based Assessment:

- Students are assessed based on their performance in project-based tasks or assignments that require them to apply STEAM concepts to solve real-world problems or challenges.
- Assessment criteria may include the quality of project outcomes, depth of understanding demonstrated, effectiveness of problem-solving strategies, creativity and innovation, collaboration and teamwork, and communication skills.

2. **Rubric-Based Evaluation:**
   - Rubrics are used to assess student work based on predefined criteria and performance levels. Rubrics can be tailored to specific STEAM projects or tasks and provide clear expectations for student performance.
   - Rubrics may assess various aspects of student work, including content knowledge, application of STEAM principles, critical thinking skills, creativity, collaboration, and communication.
3. **Portfolio Assessment:**
   - Students compile portfolios showcasing their work across different STEAM projects or activities over a period of time. Portfolios may include project reports, design sketches, prototypes, reflective journals, and multimedia artifacts.
   - Portfolios provide a comprehensive view of students' learning progression, allowing for ongoing assessment of their growth, development, and achievements in STEAM education.
4. **Performance-Based Assessment:**
   - Performance-based assessments involve observing and evaluating students as they demonstrate their skills and competencies in STEAM-related tasks or activities.
   - Assessments may include presentations, demonstrations, exhibitions, simulations, or performances that require students to apply their knowledge and skills in authentic contexts.
5. **Authentic Assessments:**
   - Authentic assessments are designed to mirror real-world tasks or challenges, allowing students to demonstrate their abilities in meaningful contexts.
   - Examples of authentic assessments in STEAM education include designing and testing prototypes, conducting experiments, solving engineering challenges, creating multimedia projects, and presenting solutions to community problems.

6. **Formative Assessment:**

- Formative assessment strategies, such as quizzes, concept maps, peer feedback, and classroom discussions, are used to monitor student progress and provide ongoing feedback.
- Formative assessment helps teachers identify areas where students may need additional support or clarification and inform instructional decisions to enhance learning outcomes in STEAM subjects.

7. **Summative Assessment:**

- Summative assessments, such as exams, standardized tests, or culminating projects, are administered at the end of a learning period to evaluate students' overall achievement in STEAM education.
- Summative assessments provide a comprehensive evaluation of students' knowledge, skills, and competencies acquired throughout a STEAM course or unit of study.

By employing a variety of assessment approaches, STEAM educators can effectively evaluate students' learning outcomes and provide meaningful feedback to support their continued growth and development in interdisciplinary fields.

PLANNER
STEAM PROJECTS

We have provided a number of sample activities for you to try out but ultimately we want you to be confident to plan your own!

The following pages are simple guidelines to help you plan, execute and evaluate your own STEAM project! Choose and match STEAM activities that are desirable, feasible and viable for you in your situation.

Before You Begin a STEAM Project it is useful to ask yourself at least some of the questions provided in our

STEAM Planning checklist on the following pages.

And we have provided a simple STEAM Canvas Tool to organise your thoughts & plans.

First we will run through some useful information about STEAM Spaces and Resources.

PLANNING STEAM PROJECTS

PHYSICAL SPACE

If you don't have a dedicated physical "STEAM" space in your school don't worry, you don't need one! There are activities and opportunities to suit all kinds of spaces, including regular classrooms.

Consider the questions about space included in our checklist in the following pages.

If it helps you can sketch out a rough blueprint of your classroom / school / surroundings to highlight the space and resources available and develop a "vision board" for STEAM activity planning.

Or jump straight into your classroom with one of the activities provided

MENTAL SPACE

Creating and allowing the mental space for relaxed and open engagement is as, if not more important as the physical space!

Time is an important element - the requirements really depend on the specific activity - but aim to have enough time that you and the students don't rush through activities, and still have time for discussion, reflection, and clean up / display.

STEAM PLANNING CHECKLIST

	PLAN ASK YOURSELF	ASPIRE AIM FOR
CHALLENGE	What are you aiming for? What kind of challenge do you want? What practices does it promote? What is the level of active learning it allows? What is its connection with the context?	Relevant, fun, authentic, achievable Include multiple parameters/levels and possibilities for success Discuss with students what they are aiming for/ what "success" might look like The process is as/more important than a specific result / outcome!
CONTEXT	What is the context? What role does it play in the project? What degree of authenticity does it allow? How does it frame the challenge? What is the motivation of the learner to engage?	Clarity, coherence, consistency Better to focus clearly on a few things /a key question or topic in depth, rather than trying to cover too much. The more relevant to the lives/aspirations of the learners the more engaged they will be!
EDUCATIONAL CONTEXT	Which learning objectives do we want to achieve? What others could be/are usefully included/applied?	Keep it simple Aim to focus on a few key objectives that engage different skills and competencies Link skills and competencies to real world applications and opportunities

& SIMPLE REFLECTION SHEET

REFLECT: How did it go in the classroom?

Super!	Very well	Ok	Not Sure	Not Well

	PLAN	ASPIRE
	ASK YOURSELF	**AIM FOR**
CONTENTS	Which content will you include in this project? How will the contents be presented? Are there any content areas missing that would support better learning and engagement? What level of depth will you go towards?	Accessible Targeted to the level(s) of the learners Allow room for meander, discussion, space to be creative, to think and process the information/activity
LOWTECH MATERIALS & RESOURCES	What kind of materials do you have easy access to? Can you use recycled/ upcycled etc materials? Do you have a budget for materials and or external expertise and support?	Aim for upcycling, recycling, re-use, re-purposing of as much as possible. There is no need to spend a lot.
ICT- TOOLS & HIGH TECH	What tools and technologies do you have access to? Which will you use? Do you have sufficient devices and	The technology and tools should be the vehicle for learning, not the purpose of the STEAM project - irrespective of whether it is a high tech activity or low tech. Poems are written with pencils not by pencils!

REFLECT: How did it go in the classroom?

Super!	Very well	Ok	Not Sure	Not Well

	PLAN	ASPIRE
	ASK YOURSELF	AIM FOR
ICT- TOOLS & HIGH TECH	expertise for each child/ group of children to participate? Why? What will they be used for? What do they promote? What do they activate? What else might do the same job?	The technology and tools should be the vehicle for learning, not the purpose of the STEAM project - irrespective of whether it is a high tech activity or low tech. Poems are written with pencils not by pencils!
PHYSICAL SPACE	What space/spaces are easily available to you & for how long? Do you plan to display or exhibit the project outcomes in the same space and leave time for other classes to visit and explore? Does your idea/project require specific materials that will affect where you do it e.g. water sources	Aim for a space that suits the activity or challenge - Any of the following will work, depending on the situation: classroom / hall / art or STEAM room/ playground / virtual spaces / other

REFLECT: How did it go in the classroom?

Super!	Very well	Ok	Not Sure	Not Well

	PLAN ASK YOURSELF	ASPIRE AIM FOR
MENTAL SPACE	This is as if not more important than the physical space! -Plan time for discussion, reflection, and clean up as well as the activity, all the elements are important, as is time to process everything	- Open minded, relaxed and open engagement - Encourage doing and thinking about things in ways that you might not normally do, looking from different perspectives -sometimes it is necessary to make a mess, or see where a tangent takes you!
CLASSROOM ACTIVITIES	What is the sequence of the activities planned? Are they following a logical process? What ways of thinking, doing or speaking will be important in the classroom?	Give yourself enough time! Time requirements really depend on the specific activity - aim to have enough time that you and the students don't rush through activities, and still have time for discussion, reflection, and clean up. Use/create an appropriate space for you and your students - physical and mental!
STEAM	What level of interdisciplinarity is the project promoting? What discipline or disciplines guide the project? Will we use S, T, E, A, M techniques and procedures?	You don't have to force in all of the S, T, E, A, M areas - integrate the disciplines / topics that are relevant to solve/address the proposed challenge.Usually, there is a discipline that acts as a leader.

REFLECT: How did it go in the classroom?

Super!	Very well	Ok	Not Sure	Not Well

TRY THIS SIMPLE STEAM

Description of Activities

Context

Educational Objectives

Context

Classroom Activities

S

T

E

PLANNING CANVAS

Low Tech Materials & Resources

ICT- Tools & High Tech

Physical Space

Mental Space

A

M

GATHER STEAM RESOURCES & SUPPORT!

STEAM SUPPORT

It's more fun and easier to make progress if you have a team / a few people to support your efforts. Consider working together with other teachers to develop and try your STEAM activities.

You might also consider working with an external partner, such as a visiting scientist / engineer / artist / tech person or organisation like a Fab Lab/Maker Space. Visiting specialists are a great way to engage the students and provide different perspectives on the activities and the possibilities for your students' future.

STEAM RESOURCES

STEAM Resources are Everywhere!

Lots of regular school supplies can be used in STEAM activities - everything in the arts and crafts department, recycling/upcycling materials, science equipment, computers etc.

High Tech STEAM activities involving computers/laptops/tablets and/or technical equipment

such as soldering tools, glue guns etc. might require the use of a computer lab or a specifically designed area such as a "maker space" type area.

Example 1: you are planning a once off project/lesson/activity, you only have a couple of hours, you need something very easy to set up and remove - this will inform your space and materials choices [don't use e.g. slow dry paints, or clays; don't start with high tech; go for no-tech/low tech/simple materials -if it goes well you build on it for the next activity/plan]

Example 2: you are planning a longer running project that you want to come back to periodically, leaving the materials/resources in place, with the longer term idea of an exhibition of some kind

-this will inform your space and materials choices in different ways [ideally a more open, art room type space, water supply, space/ facilities to leave paint/glue/clay etc to dry]

STEAM RESOURCES

Low Tech/No Tech

"No-Tech" Options include Arts'n'Crafts materials, materials from the recycling bin, re-usable/ upcycled materials and "regular" day-to-day school supplies.

"Low-Tech & Tinkering"

Tinkering is a form of informal learning based on learning by doing, using low tech tools combined with recycled materials, paper, plastic and wood. Tinkering allows children to learn to experiment and play games, while developing skills such as problem solving and team work. You can easily and quickly build objects, design creative products that move, draw or float, explore different materials, work with mechanical elements or gears, create simple functioning and luminous electrical circuits, and much more.

Examples of low tech materials:

Batteries, magnets, 3V electric motors, electric/copper wire or sticky copper tape, alligator clips, LEDs, playdoh/ paper/ potatoes can all be used to make e.g. simple circuits, without any great expense or technical expertise.

Add a glue gun / insulating tape / blue tack / straws / large plastic caps /wooden sticks/skewers / rubber bands / empty plastic bottles / scissors / pliers and more to make electrical circuits, small robots, mechanical toys, marble tracks, chain reaction mechanisms, sculptures. The possibilities are endless!

STEAM RESOURCES

Where to Start with High Tech

Don't be afraid! You can start trying out high tech activities in your classroom without much if any expense, depending on the equipment you already have - e.g. tablets, phone and laptops can all be used to run easy to use free or affordable software to help you try activities involving fun techie activities such as Coding, 3D modelling, Stop-motion animation/ storytelling with software, and simple soldering for electronic circuits.

-Try coding with your class with Scratch Jr., Lightbot

-Tell stories with Puppet Pals, use Book Creator or any Stop Motion app.

-If you have access to 'Lego We Do' you can also let them code to different subject related contents. In combination with lego brick building, reading stories and collaborating with a partner this is a lot of fun.

-If you have robots like Dash or Bluebot for example, then you can let your pupils learn to read and understand and collaborate while programming the robot.

-Start 3D modelling [easy with Laptops, WLAN & Tinkercad]

-No tablets, no Laptops no problem! You can do some coding with Bluebot / Beebot so you can work with 6 groups in the class.

All of these activities encourage and engage pupils to collaborate, build, create, measure, code, exchange ideas and in the end do a presentation in front of the others showing the processes they went through, what difficulties they had programming it, what ideas they elaborated together and so on.

ENGAGE WITH STEAM ACTIVITIES

Juice-Pouch Stomp Rocket

This rocket from Ana Dziengel of Babble Dabble Doo uses the power of compressed air to launch into the sky. (Budding engineers take note: This is called pneumatics!)

What You'll Need:

1. Empty juice pouch
2. One flexible straw (that comes with the pouch)
3. One standard straw
4. Colored cardstock
5. Washi tape (optional)
6. Modeling clay and scissor

What To Do:

1. Snip off the end of the flexible straw on an angle.
2. Insert the pointed end of the straw into the straw hole of the juice pouch.
3. Cut the second straw in half. This will be your rocket.
4. Make three trapezoids from cardstock, in the following dimensions: 3 inches (base) x 1 inch (height) x 3/4 inches (top). Set two aside to be full fins. Cut the last one in half vertically.
5. Tape the full fins on each side of the straw. Don't flatten the straw.
6. Tape one half-fin perpendicularly to each full fin as shown. Add washi tape to decorate the straw if desired.
7. Roll a small bit of clay into a ball. Add this to the top to seal the straw completely.
8. To launch the rocket, inflate the pouch by blowing into the flexible straw. Bend the flexible straw to aim and place the rocket straw over the end. Stomp down hard for liftoff!

Note: If after some use, one of the straws cracks, simply replace it with a new one.

Pom-Pom Catapult

This simple machine uses stored energy (the tension in the rubber bands) to release a projectile (called the payload).

What You'll Need:

1. Hole punch
2. Rectangular box
3. Three unsharpened pencils
4. A few strong rubber bands
5. Masking tape or glue
6. Jar lid and paper clip

What To Do:

1. Punch a hole in a long side of the box, 3 inches from a short side.
2. Punch a matching hole on the other side. The holes should be large to rotate a pencil easily. Punch a third hole on the opposite side; it should be centered and near the bottom.
3. Assemble the catapult arm: Join 2 pencils together perpendicularly to make an inverted lowercase t; secure them with rubber bands.
4. Tape or glue a small jar lid to the longer end of the arm
5. Wrap another rubber band around the shorter end of the arm using a slipknot.
6. Place the ends of the horizontal pencil in the side holes.
7. Thread the tail of the slipknot (from Step 4) through the remaining hole, and knot a paper clip around the end to hold it in place.
8. Create a "stopper" for the catapult arm with the third pencil. Place it across the top of the box just in front of the arm; secure it in place by wrapping a large rubber band around one end of the pencil, under the box, and up and around the other end. Load it up, and let 'er fly.

Electric Play-Doh Lightning Bug

In this STEAM activity, kids will create a simple closed circuit to make their bug glow.

What You'll Need:

1. Cardstock
2. Play-Doh
3. 10mm diffused LED bulb with leads
4. Four AA batteries
5. Four AA battery pack with leads
6. Scissors

What To Do:

1. Cut an oval cardstock base for the bug and two heart-shaped wings.
2. From Play-Doh, make the head and two separate, oblong sides; place them on the paper base. (Make sure the side pieces don't touch each other or the bug won't light up.)
3. Add eyes and antennae as you like.
4. Look at the leads of the LED. The longer one is the positive lead, and the shorter one is the negative.
5. Pull the leads apart, and stick one end into each side of the body. Remember which side has the positive lead.
6. Insert the batteries into the battery pack. Stick the red wire into the side with the positive LED lead; put the black wire into the other.
7. Turn on the battery pack and watch the bug glow!

Note: If your bug doesn't light up, turn the LED around and insert the long lead into the other side of the body.

Balance Sculpture

Your budding builders will need to be patient as they test to find the sweet spot to make it balance!

What You'll Need:

1. Cardboard
2. Craft paint
3. Paper-towel tube
4. 5-inch square piece of cardboard
5. Hot glue
6. Scissors
7. Floral wire or pipe cleaners
8. Beads
9. 12-inch bamboo skewer with sharp ends snipped off

What To Do:

1. Cut the cardboard into shapes; paint. Paint the paper-towel tube and square piece of cardboard. Let dry.
2. Flatten one end of the paper-towel tube; staple closed. Cut a small V-shaped notch in the center of the flattened end. This will be the fulcrum.
3. Glue the open end of the paper-towel tube to the cardboard square (adult supervision needed). Let dry.
4. Thread cardboard shapes, wire, and beads onto a long skewer, balancing and adjusting it on the notch.
5. Continue adjusting, using tape if needed for security, until the sculpture is balanced.

Invisible Ink

When life gives you lemons, make a secret message from invisible ink!

What You'll Need:

1. One lemon
2. Cotton swab
3. Sheet of white paper
4. Sunlight, iron, or lightbulb

What To Do:

1. Squeeze the lemon juice into a bowl and add a spoonful of water.
2. Mix gently. Dip the swab into the liquid and write a message or draw a picture on the paper.
3. Let the liquid dry completely so that the message or picture is invisible. To share your secret, set it in sunlight, hold it close to a lightbulb, or iron (with adult help).
4. The message will be revealed! Hang it as artwork, or share it with a friend.

How Does It Work?

Diluting or adding water to the lemon juice makes it very hard to see when you apply it to the paper, but lemon juice is an organic substance that oxidizes and turns brown when it's heated up. This means that no one will notice that the secret is there until the paper is heated and the message is revealed! Other substances that work in the same way include orange juice, honey diluted with water, milk, onion juice, and vinegar.

Solar System

This far-out felting project is to get the kids psyched to go back to science class.

What You'll Need:

1. About 2 oz of 100% wool roving in assorted colors
2. Two 38-gauge star-point felting needles (adult supervision needed)
3. Felting pad or dense foam
4. White fiberfill stuffing
5. White paint and Two paint-stirring sticks
6. Drill and 3/32-inch drill bit (adult supervision needed)
7. White baker's twine or thin cotton yarn
8. Sewing needle with a large eye
9. Brass fish-eye hook
10. Small brass chain

Solar System

What To Do:

1. To make a planet, pull off a few inches of roving and roll it into a ball so it fits in your palm.
2. Pin onto the felt pad with one needle and use the other to "felt," or to press the needle up and down repeatedly. The tiny barbs on the end of the felting needle compress the fibers into a desired shape.
3. Turn the roving often and continue felting until it forms a semi-firm and uniform ball. Felt on a thin piece of roving in a different color if desired (to make the blue swirls on Neptune, for instance). Repeat to make additional planets.
4. To make the sun, pull a 4- to 5-inch-diameter tuft of stuffing and wrap it with yellow roving to cover stuffing completely.
5. Paint two paint-stirring sticks and let dry. Mark five holes, spaced about 3 inches apart, on one of the paint sticks. Drill. Place the drilled stick over the other one as a template, mark holes, and drill.
6. With the sticks in an "X" shape, line up the center holes; use the needle to thread the sun through the center hole. Knot to desired length.
7. Twist in the fish-eye hook from the top to secure the paint sticks together. Secure the planets to yarn with the needle and thread up through remaining eight holes.
8. Knot in place at desired heights. Add a chain to hang; felt on small amounts of wool to planets as needed to balance the mobile.

Bath Bombs

Scrub-a-dub-dub! Add some science to the tub with these pretty and so-simple bath bombs from Curious Jane.

What You'll Need:

1. 1/2 cup citric acid, 1 cup baking soda
2. 1/2 cup cornstarch, 1/2 cup Epsom salt
3. Essential oil of your choice,1 tsp water, 1 tsp olive oil
4. Sphere-shaped mold (we used clear plastic ornaments)

What To Do:

1. Combine citric acid, baking soda, cornstarch, and Epsom salt in a large bowl. Mix well and set aside. In a small bowl, mix together one or two drops of essential oil, water, and olive oil.
2. Add the wet mixture to the dry very slowly. Mix it together quickly and thoroughly so it doesn't begin to bubble.
3. Once it's all combined, let the mixture sit for a few minutes; it should look and feel like wet sand. If it's still too dry, add a drop of olive oil, but don't oversaturate.
4. Separate the mixture into smaller bowls and add food coloring, mixing in the color by hand.
5. Layer the different colors in both halves of a sphere-shaped mold and pack them down. When each side is completely filled with a slight mound, press them together and gently rotate until the sides lock.
6. Let the bomb dry in the mold for a few minutes, then carefully remove the top half. Leave it for another hour or two, then carefully turn the bottom half out of the mold.
7. Let it dry overnight.

Dancing Puppet

Surprise: The whole robot moves with the pull of a string!

What You'll Need:

1. Paint and paintbrush
2. A piece of cardboard cut into 13 strips that are 1½-inch-wide (four 10-inch pieces, four 5-inch pieces, one 4-inch piece, and four 3½-inch pieces)
3. Construction paper
4. Pencil
5. Scissors
6. Hole punch
7. 1-inch-capacity brads
8. Glue
9. 6-inch piece of string

What To Do:

1. Paint one side of each cardboard piece black; let dry. Trace the robot-face template onto construction paper and cut out; fold as directed.
2. Following the template, punch holes in the cardboard pieces and connect the face and cardboard pieces with brads.
3. Score the 4-inch piece of cardboard into sections, then fold it into a T and glue it to the back of the puppet; let dry.
4. Tie the string to the bottom-most brad.
5. Hold the puppet by the handle and pull on the string to get the arms and legs moving.

Pentominoes

Pentominoes are shapes made from groups of congruent squares.

What You'll Need:

1. Glue
2. 60 unfinished 1-inch wooden cubes (we got ours on amazon.com)
3. Paintbrush
4. Paint in color(s) of your choice

What To Do:

1. Sort the wooden cubes into groups of five, then challenge your child to create 12 different shapes where each cube .
2. Share atleast one side with another. These are your pentominoes! (Use the photo as a key if they get stuck.)
3. Once your child has found all 12 configurations, glue the cubes together and paint them as desired. (We mixed teal with increasing amounts of white paint for an ombré set.)
4. Time to play! Have your child try to create various squares and rectangles with the blocks. (Hint: They'll need four different puzzle pieces to complete a 4 x 5 rectangle.)

Math Fact Triangles

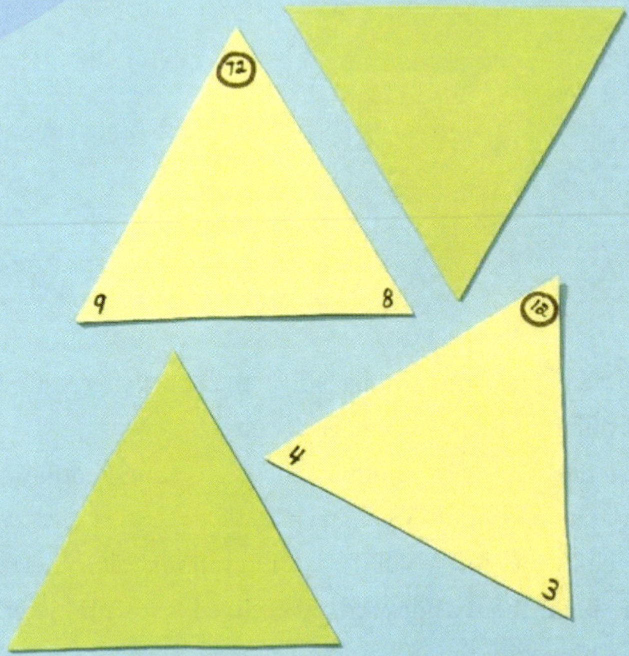

Most parents learned to solve problems in a linear way: 1 + 2 = 3. Using the triangles helps kids think in "fact families." They learn that 1 + 2 = 3 and 3 - 2 = 1 at the same time.

What You'll Need:

1. Craft foam in various colors
2. Scissors
3. Sharpie pen

What To Do:

1. Cut out equal-sized triangles from different colors of craft foam.
2. Along with your child, use a Sharpie to write an addition/subtraction or multiplication/division equation (depending on your child's skills) on each triangle, placing one number in each corner; circle the answer.
3. Flip the triangles over. Choose one, cover the circled answer with your finger, and ask your child to solve it. (To practice the opposite operation, cover one of the other numbers.)

Perler Bead Arrays

Take a break from flash cards and practice multiplication tables using arrays, which allow kids to see the answers as they study.

What You'll Need:

1. Perler beads (we got ours from Amazon)
2. Perler beads clear square pegboards (such as this set)
3. Iron

What To Do:

1. Write out an equation (say, 7 x 3), then challenge your child to express it with Perler beads as an array of three columns of seven.
2. Then count the total number of beads to figure out the answer.
3. If your child is struggling with particular equations or a line on their multiplication tables, create a permanent version for them to use: For each equation (7 x 1, 7 x 2, etc), have your child help you assemble the correct number of beads into an array (so one column of seven, two columns of seven, etc.), then (with your assistance) iron to set according to package directions.
4. Break them out whenever they need some practice.

DIY Scratch Paper

This STEAM activity for kids involves making your own color-scratch cards and sending a magical message.

What You'll Need:

1. Blank white cards
2. Crayons
3. Masking tape
4. 2 tbsp clear detergent
5. 2 tbsp black acrylic paint
6. Paintbrush
7. Small plastic mixing bowl
8. Spoon

What To Do:

1. Tape down the card with masking tape around the edges.
2. Color in completely with a rainbow of crayons.
3. Mix the black acrylic paint and clear detergent in a small bowl.
4. Paint the card with the mixture, and allow it to dry. Do at least two coats.
5. When completely dry, slowly and carefully peel the masking tape away. Scratch your message into the card with a
6. Coin or the pointed end of the paintbrush, and see the colors revealed!

DIY Ice-Cream

In this STEAM activity for kids, you'll make ice cream by surrounding the ingredients with a layer of even colder ice.

What You'll Need:

1. One quart-sized zip-top bag
2. One gallon-sized zip-top bag
3. 4 cups ice
4. 6 tbsp rock salt
5. 1/2 cup half-and-half
6. 1 tbsp vanilla extract
7. 1 tbsp white sugar

What To Do:

1. Add the ice and rock salt to the gallon-sized bag. Shake to coat.
2. Combine half-and-half, sugar, extract, and a pinch of salt in the quart-sized bag. Seal it tight, getting all the air out.
3. Nestle the small bag of ice cream mixture into the large bag of ice, so that the ice surrounds it. Seal the large bag tightly.
4. Now shake, shake, shake it up! After about 5 minutes, your sweet treat will be ready to eat!

Sand Pendulum

This STEAM activity for kids creates a pendulum—essetially a weight that hangs freely from a string

What You'll Need:

1. Yarn
2. Scissors
3. Sturdy rubber band
4. Kitchen funnel
5. Broomstick or dowel
6. Poster paper (to catch the sand)
7. Craft sand

What To Do:

1. Cut three lengths of yarn, each about 3 inches long. Tie each piece to the rubber band, spacing them equally apart Slip the rubber band over the funnel so that it fits tightly under the lip.
2. Gather the strings above the funnel and tie them at the top so that the funnel hangs evenly.
3. Suspend the funnel from a broomstick or dowel (or just hold it). Place paper below to catch the sand.
4. Have your child fill the funnel with sand, blocking the small opening of the funnel with their finger as they fill it.

Instruct them to remove their finger and give it a little push.

Balancing Buddy

When completing this STEAM activity, your student will be delighted to see this silly pal teeter on its tiny toothpick point!

What You'll Need:

1. Wine cork
2. Two 12-inch bamboo skewers
3. Toothpick
4. Modeling clay
5. Decorations (like paper, googly eyes, and paint)

What To Do:

1. Place the cork upright on your work surface. Press the pointy end of a skewer into one side of the cork at a 45-degree angle (the ends should point up); repeat on the opposite side. Press the toothpick into the top center of the cork.
2. Roll two equal-size balls of modeling clay and press them onto the ends of the skewers. Decorate the cork as desired.
3. Place the tip of the toothpick on your finger to see if the toy balances. If it leans to one side, adjust the angles of the skewers until it stands up straight.

How Does It Work?

Every object has a center of gravity—the point where its mass is evenly distributed. Because the clay balls are heavier than the cork, they bring the center of gravity to the bottom of the toothpick. In order for the toy to "stand," the weight of the balls must also be in balance. Adjusting the skewers helps to compensate for any difference in size and allows Buddy to stay centered.

Brushbot

This crazy critter moves on its own. Just don't expect it to clean the floors!

What You'll Need:

1. Four AA batteries
2. 6-volt battery case with wire lead terminals and an on-off switch
3. 6-volt hobby motor
4. Washer, dime, or other small, flat object
5. Kitchen brush , electric tape and Duct tape
6. Felt
7. ScissorsTacky glue

What To Do:

1. Put batteries in the battery case.
2. Connect the leads to the hobby motor (it doesn't matter which color lead connects to which), and secure the wires in place with electrical tape.
3. Attach the washer to the motor's shaft with electrical tape.
4. Attach the battery pack and motor to the brush with duct tape, and decorate as desired (just make sure you can still access the on-off switch).
5. Turn it on to see it move on its bristle "feet."

How Does It Work?

This STEAM activity for kids creates a simple circuit, a closed path that an electrical current travels through. The battery provides the electricity, and the wires conduct it to the motor. When the motor's shaft spins, the washer throws it off-balance, making the whole motor—and the brush along with it—vibrate and move.

Zip-Line Toy Transporter

Get gravity working to move toys—quickly!—from one side of the room to the other in this nifty rocket ship.

What You'll Need:

1. Cardboard tea box
2. Removable adhesive wall hook (like a Command Hook)
3. Hole punch , Cardstock and Swivel-eye pulley
4. Scissors, Duct Tape and Tacky glue
5. 11 ½ feet of parachute cord, cut into two pieces (10 feet and 16 inches)

What To Do:

1. Attach the hook to a wall, about as high as your child can reach; let set.
2. Cut the box in half lengthwise, punch holes in two opposite sides, then use our template to create the rocket from cardstock and adhere it to the box.
3. Tie one end of the 16-inch rope to one hole, loop it through the eye of the pulley, and tie it to the hole on the other side.
4. Run the 10-foot piece of rope through the block (wheel) of the pulley. Tie a loop onto one end, then hang it on the wall hook.
5. Pull the other end of the rope until it's taut, then use duct tape to secure it to the floor at a 45-degree angle from the wall (or hold it in place for your child).
6. Have your child push the rocket all the way up to the top of the line, then let go and watch the rocket fly!

How Does It Work?

The far end of the rope is lower than the anchor point in the wall, gravity pulls the rocket toward the ground—super fast!

Yardstick Launcher

Lightweight balls, toys, and other objects toward a target across the room with the stomp of a foot with this STEAM activity.

What You'll Need:

1. Hot glue
2. Clean metal can (like a coffee can)
3. Scrapbook paper,Tape and Yardstick
4. Acrylic paint and paintbrush
5. Four plastic party cups and Rubberband
6. Ping-pong balls or other small objects

What To Do:

1. Cover the can with scrapbook paper and secure with tape. Paint the yardstick; let dry.
2. Use hot glue to attach the plastic party cups to one end of the yardstick (an adult's job). Secure the can to the middle of the yardstick with a rubber band.
3. Place ping-pong balls or other small objects in the cups, then stomp or quickly press down on the free end of the yardstick to launch the projectiles across the room.

How Does It Work?

A lever is a simple machine made from a rigid beam (the yardstick) and a fulcrum (the can). When your child applies downward force to one side, it elicits an opposite reaction, sending the unattached load (the ping-pong balls) flying. You can change the amount of effort it takes to move those balls: The closer the can is to the cups, the less work it takes to move the projectiles.

Cloud in a Jar

This homemade rainstorm project from Curious Jane teaches your student about weather systems and precipitation.

What You'll Need:

1. Jar and Water
2. Shaving cream and Food coloring
3. Medicine dropper

What To Do:

1. Fill the jar with water until it is almost full.
2. Squirt foam shaving cream over the top, so it completely covers the surface.
3. Fill a small cup with water and add plenty of blue food coloring.
4. Using a medicine dropper, have your child dribble blue water on top of the shaving-cream cloud, and watch the rainstorm form.

Suspension Bridge

With this STEAM activity for kids from Curious Jane, your little architect can design and build a bridge, where the deck is supported by cables.

What You'll Need:

1. Heavy books
2. Six to 10 foam boards, each 8 inches by 10 inches
3. Duct tape and Two chairs
4. Scissors and Thick and thin cord

What To Do:

1. Tape foam boards together lengthwise to form the deck. Punch holes at the end corners, as shown.
2. Span the deck from one chair seat to the other. Set heavy books on each end to weight the deck.
3. Cut two lengths of thick cord, about twice as long as the distance between the tops of the chairs; these will be the suspension cables. Rig the cables over the chairs as shown below, tying them to punched holes at each end.
4. Cut a piece of thin cord for the center vertical cable. Tie it to the midpoint of one suspension cable. Loop it under the deck and up the other side; tie this to the midpoint of the other suspension cable so that the deck is supported.
5. Follow the same process as above, securing the vertical cables on either side of the center cable.
6. Keep placing cables until they reach the towers and the deck is fully supported. Your child will need to tweak and adjust cord placement as they go.
7. Have your kid test how much the bridge can hold—they'll be amazed!

"Tie-Dye" Pillows

This STEAM project is a mini-lesson in solubility Permanent marker doesn't wash away with water. However, the molecules in the ink are soluble in rubbing alcohol, so the ink spreads to make a pretty pattern.

What You'll Need:

1. Dryer
2. Permanent markers in various colors
3. White polypropylene pillow insert
4. Medicine dropper and Rubbing alcohol

What To Do:

1. Have your kid draw with permanent markers on one side of the pillow insert. (Don't forget to protect the work surface! The more ink they use, the more the color will bleed.)
2. When your kid is done drawing, have them use a medicine dropper to dribble alcohol onto the pillow and watch the magic happen.
3. To finish, let it dry and run it through the dryer on high heat to seal in the design.

Exploding Baggie

See science in action when vinegar (an acid) and baking soda (a base) combine to create carbon dioxide—a gas that inflates and causes its container to burst!

What You'll Need:

1. 1/2 cup vinegar
2. Gallon-sized zip-top bag
3. Food coloring
4. Binder clip
5. 1/4 cup baking soda
6. Safety goggles

What To Do:

1. Put on safety goggles.
2. Pour vinegar into the zip-top bag and add a drop or two of food coloring.
3. Twist the baggie just above the liquid and secure it with a binder clip, leaving space at the top.
4. Add the baking soda to the top portion of the bag. Seal tight!
5. Set outside or on a covered table. Have paper towels handy!
6. Remove the clip, allowing the baking soda and vinegar to combine. (Give a little shake if needed.)
7. Step back, and watch it inflate…and explode!

Meyer Lemon Volcanoes

A little mashing and a lot of fizz makes a mini volcano in this STEAM experiment! The citric acid of the lemon juice reacts with the baking soda to release carbon dioxide gas, fizz, and foam.

What You'll Need:

1. Two lemons
2. 1 tbsp baking soda
3. One drop Dawn dish soap
4. Food coloring (optional)
5. Plate, knife, fork, and cup

What To Do:

1. Slice a bit off the bottom of the first lemon (so it will sit flat) and remove a core from the top.
2. Halve and juice the second lemon, and set it aside.
3. Set the cored lemon on a plate, and mush the inside with a fork. Make sure to keep all the lemon juice in the lemon; it's important for the reaction.
4. Squeeze a few drops of food coloring (if desired) and a few drops of Dawn dish soap into the lemon.
5. Add a spoonful of baking soda into the lemon (it should start to fizz), and mush with the fork—it should start foaming and bubbling!
6. Keep the reaction going by adding more baking soda, dish soap, and reserved lemon juice.

STEAM

SUCCESSES EVALUATE & CELEBRATE

It is important to reflect on and assess your STEAM activities, to get the most out of them for yourself and your students. We invite you, as teachers who are new to STEAM, to participate in our Evaluation of this STEAM H project overall and this particular output!
We hope that you enjoy it and that you will provide us with valu- able feedback to ensure that primary teachers are as well support- ed as we can manage in this project.

There are two options:

Option 1: DIY - Choose an activity, test it with your class, and use the simplified planning, reflection and evaluation sheets to reflect on your efforts!

Option 2: Participate in our more comprehensive evaluation of the activities, the Handbook, and the relevance and use of this STEAM project overall to you and your students.

We would be very grateful for your participation. The evaluation sheet for the more comprehensive evaluation is available here - you can fill it in online or download and submit.

EVALUATING HOW WELL STEAM ACTIVITIES

OBSERVATION OF STUDENTS	EVALUATION OF THE LEVEL ACHIEVED	
DIMENSIONS	**Advanced**	**Intermediate**
CHALLENGE: Understanding and managing the challenge	Students understand and autonomously manage the challenge and perform it well, even in new situations /with new parameters added	Students understand and autonomously manage the challenge and performing well
CONTENT & CONTEXT: Understanding the content, context and being motivated to learn	Students understand the content and context very well, are motivated to learn and seek additional information and challenges	Students understand the content and context well, were well motivated to learn
LITERACY: Knowing and using specific vocabulary: -use appropriate language -organise information in coherent texts and diagrams	Students understand and use the vocabulary specific to the discipline[s] very well, arrange the materials with awareness, and communicative effectiveness.	Students understand and use the vocabulary specific to the discipline[s] well, arrange the materials with awareness, and communicative effectiveness.

BY STUDENTS IN THE CLASSROOM		NOTES
Basic	Initial acquisition	Aditional Comments
Students understand and manage the challenge and show competence in carrying out the basic steps.	Students understand and manages the basic challenge with support	
Students understand the content and context well, and were motivated to learn	Students understand the basic content and context and were motivated to learn with support	
Students understand and use the vocabulary specific to the discipline[s] to some extent	Students need help to understand and use the vocabulary specific to the discipline[s] and relationship to materials and how to communicate	

OBSERVATION OF STUDENTS	EVALUATION OF THE LEVEL ACHIEVED	
DIMENSIONS	**Advanced**	**Intermediate**
LEARNING OBJECTIVES	All Learning Objectives were achieved to a high degree	All/most Learning Objectives were achieved quite well
MATERIALS & RESOURCES: -analyse and choose materials to be used -make informed choices relevant to the task	Students identify and select information and materials autonomously and confidently, making informed choices.	Students Identify and select information and materials autonomously.
ICT - TOOLS & HIGH TECH: Knowing and using the main computer, ICT Tools, apps and multimedia procedures relevant to the task	Students autonomously and consciously use the ICT tools and apps relevant to the task, confidently use them at the basic level directed, and pursue further knowledge, applications, tools etc	Students autonomously and consciously use the ICT tools and apps relevant to the task

BY STUDENTS IN THE CLASSROOM		NOTES
Basic	Initial acquisition	Aditional Comments
All / most Learning Objectives were achieved well	Most Learning Objectives were achieved to some degree	
Students Identify and select only some information autonomously.	Students identify and select some information and/ or materials with the support of a guide.	
Students use the ICT tools and apps relevant to the task, but need the teacher's help in the personal revision phase.	Students use the ICT tools and apps relevant to the task, but nNeed constant guidance from the teacher throughout	

OBSERVATION OF STUDENTS	EVALUATION OF THE LEVEL ACHIEVED	
DIMENSIONS	**Advanced**	**Intermediate**
CREATIVITY SKILLS:	Students approach activities challenges in interesting, innovative and creative ways, that are original to them, & go beyond the basic instructions	Students approach activities challenges in creative ways, with original aspects
SPEAKING IN PUBLIC: -master communication techniques -control emotionality -solve the unexpected	Students handle communication independently and confidently. Are in full control of emotions and able to resolve unforeseen situations promptly	Students handle communication/ presentation independently. Control emotions and resolve unforeseen circumstances
COLLABORATION SKILLS: Learning together: -respect tasks, roles and time -support and listen to others -collaborate	Students respect tasks, roles and times, support the work of others, promote cooperation and listen to everyone. Support the group in a proactive way	Students respect tasks, roles and times, collaborate and listen actively.
STEAM:	Students understand links, overlap of subjects, broader context and seek further information	Students understand links, overlap of subjects, broader context

BY STUDENTS IN THE CLASSROOM		NOTES
Basic	**Initial acquisition**	**Aditional Comments**
Students engage in creative skills and will push the boundaries with encouragement and assistance from teacher	Students need a constant encouragement to go beyond basic creative skills	
Students manage communication and presentation well and control emotions, with some assistance	Students need support to manage their communication and presentation skills	
With somoe difficulty students respect tasks, roles and times; not very active in collaborating and listening.	Students take a passive and unproductive attitude. Need guidance to meet commitments and work with others	
Students understand some links and overlap of subjects, and broader context with some assistance	Students need assistance to understand links, overlap of subjects, and broader context	

Your Worksheet